LIFE ON ENCINITAS

Memoirs of a childhood in a small foothill town of Southern California during the 1950's and 60's

Sharon Hammond Nordstrom

Copyright © 2013 Sharon Hammond Nordstrom
All rights reserved.

ISBN: 1492935476
ISBN 13: 9781492935476
Library of Congress Control Number: 2013919233
CreateSpace Independent Publishing Platform
North Charleston, South Carolina

dedication:

To family
And to friends
Who have become
Like family

> But especially
> To Kelly,
> Whom I pray
> Will delight
> In special
> Childhood
> Memories
> Of her own

> And in memory
> Of Doug,
> A precious son
> And brother

contents

A Little Background	1
In the Beginning	3
Our House	5
Summer Days and Halloween	9
Elderly People	11
More Elderly People	13
Marbles	15
Yo-yos	17
Jacks	19
Toot, Toot, Jingle, Jingle, Ding Dong	21
Saturday Matinees	23
The Big M	25
The Happiest Place on Earth	27
Hidden Valley	31
Lifesavers	35
Clifton Junior High School	37
Mother	39
Father	41
Brother Tim	43
Brother Bill	47
Extended Family	51
Everyone Goes to Church	55
Four Close Friends	57
Boyfriends	63
A Note from the Author	67

a little background

In 1950 my parents, Ralph and Laurie Hammond, emigrated from Victoria, British Columbia and settled in Monrovia, California. My brothers, Bill and Tim, were about five and six years old; Mother was newly pregnant with me.

They left Victoria for a better life via ferry to Vancouver, British Columbia. From there they caught the midnight train out of Vancouver to Portland, Oregon. After staying one night in a hotel, they boarded a Southern Pacific train to Los Angeles arriving on a cold rainy day in February. My brother Tim recalls being certain, the family was lost as they stood alone on a corner across from Union Station and Olvera Street in downtown Los Angeles. A taxi was summoned, and the four were driven to a modest auto court called the Spic and Span Motel in El Monte. After a two-week stay there, Father bought an old used car and my parents purchased a house in Monrovia for $6,900.

The purpose of the move was not only to seek a better way of life—jobs were scarce at this time in Victoria— but to reconnect with Father's sisters who lived in Southern California. They persuaded Father that a move to California would be best for the entire family. The main reason my aunts had moved from Canada was to help care for my paternal grandfather, John William Parke Hammond, who was recuperating from tuberculosis at Pottenger's Sanatorium located in the canyon above Monrovia. Recovering in the clean fresh air was by recommendation from Grandfather's doctor in Alberta, Canada. I never knew my paternal grandfather, as he passed away before I was born.

Father and Mother were vetted by the United States before they could enter the country to show they would not be a burden on the government, had money and possessed skills. After settling in Monrovia, Tim and Bill were enrolled in Mayflower Elementary School, and my parents enrolled in citizenship classes at Monrovia High School. They studied the American constitution and this country's history. Soon my parents became U.S. citizens. Tim and Bill became automatic citizens but at the age of eighteen were required to take an oath at the Los Angeles Federal Courthouse.

Life on Encinitas is a compilation of memories told through innocent young eyes from childhood through high school. I treasure the relationships and experiences with dear friends as well as the many attributes my family members passed on to me. Their love, patience, honesty, integrity and strong work ethic influence me still to this day. This memoir is a tribute to all of them.

in the beginning

My aunties, Olla, Doris, Retta and Retta's husband, my uncle Bill, are convinced I am going to die. This is their story. I am a sick baby with asthma and eczema so severe that Mother and Father must place cardboard cylinders on my arms and legs to prevent me from scratching. They roll up and store away the wool rugs transported down from Victoria, because crawling on them makes me wheeze. Father paces back and forth comforting me in an upright position on his shoulder, because the steam from the potatoes Mother is boiling in the kitchen produce a severe asthma attack. It seems I am allergic to *everything*. Surely, I am going to die.

I recall Dr. Small coming to our house on Encinitas. I am four years old. He is making a home visit to give me an injection. First, I hide under the sink, but Mother says, "I see you, Sharon." Then I hide under the dining room table with the draped tablecloth shielding me from view, but my efforts fail. Dr. Small and Mother find me, and I get a nasty shot and teaspoon of the foulest syrup. It helps me breathe.

During the next episode, Father drives me to Dr. Small's office in Pasadena. Another shot, another teaspoon of ugly taste, but at least I get a lime sucker this time. Mother proceeds to call all over Southern California to find a cure. Then she announces to Father, "Ralph, I've had an epiphany! Sharon needs to be put on raw milk!" Therefore, every few days, the milkman places raw milk on our front porch along with the regular milk. All Mother has to do is write a list of the milk she needs, roll it up with the dollar bills and set it on the front porch with the empty milk bottles the night before the morning delivery. My family loves to drink milk with every meal. I think it must be because we are Canadians.

Auntie Olla, Auntie Doris, Auntie Retta and Uncle Bill say I have eczema from my head down to my toes. Special baths, special lotions and the cardboard tubing for my arms and legs are supposed to help. They help a bit, but I still itch, scratch and wheeze all the way through high school. Often I soak my hands in a solution to dry out my skin. The concoction turns my skin a wrinkly yellowish brown, and I am so embarrassed to go to school the next day.

I am in shock when one day a classmate named James asks, "How are your hands, Sharon?" No one has *ever* asked me this before. His concern seems so sincere. James is smart and kind, and his mother is smart and lovely. She writes our school anthem, "Dear Mayflower School."

Anyway, I do not die. Mother prepares the few foods that help lessen the wheezing and itching. Father walks me upright on his shoulder between the living and dining rooms when necessary, and my brothers take turns getting up on school nights to walk and soothe me. I somehow make it, but to this day, I continue to cope with bouts of asthma and itchy sensitive skin.

our house

Our house is easy to find. It's the green bungalow halfway up the block—the one with the orange tree with its trunk painted white.

Our house is easy to find. It's the house with a trellis of tiny pink roses covering the grass and gravel driveway.

Our house is easy to find. It's the one with two pillars of huge rocks standing at attention on each side of the porch.

The house on Encinitas is my home for fourteen years. I am so happy when Della moves to our block. I am in third grade, and finally there is another girl on our street! Della is two years older, but that doesn't matter. Doug, Jimmy, Billy, Dale, Bobby and Johnny are my age and have been my only playmates for as long as I can remember. They are the boys with whom I play hide-and-go-seek, kick the can and kickball in the street. Della is ten. Her family moves from Altadena to Monrovia. She has four older brothers and a sister named Anita.

Doug has blond hair and his mom Dolores is the first mom on our block to get a *real* job. She is a checker at a huge new grocery store on Foothill Boulevard. "Oh my," says Mother when she hears about Dolores working outside the home. I think she secretly desires she could work outside the home as well.

Jimmy has brown hair and a little brother named David. We play on his swing set in the backyard. His mom and dad remind me of Beaver's parents, Ward and June Cleaver, everyone's favorite television parents.

Then there is Billy. One day, Billy's mother sends him to his room. He decides to jump out his bedroom window so he can be with his friends. On the way down, he scrapes his back on the water spigot. The trail of blood oozing down his back is quite traumatic for all of us who witness this harrowing escape. "Ugh," we all cry and our shouts alert his mother who puts Billy in the car and speeds to the hospital.

Dale has beautiful dark curly hair. He has no brothers or sisters, but his Aunt Hattie lives behind his house in a little attached apartment. I walk up the street to their house one afternoon with a new record. "I want you to hear this funny story that has been playing on the radio," I say with excitement. I share my new 45-RPM record entitled "I Am an Astronaut." I think it cost ninety-eight cents. It is an interview with Jose Jimenez, a fictional character created by comedian Bill Dana about his spaceman experience. Dale and I, along with his parents, laugh and laugh as we listen to it repeatedly.

Bobby and Johnny are brothers. Their mom is Rosemary, and she is the first mom on our street to get a driver's license. One day, we all pile into her big blue car and travel down Rosemead Boulevard to reach Long Beach. I have never been to the beach. "How much longer?" we all ask anxiously. "Are we almost there?" we whine from the back seat. Finally, we reach the ocean. The silky sand feels funny squishing between our toes. It is warm, sandy and windy; we get lots of sand in our hair and ears as we build sand castles for the first time.

Then one day Rosemary announces, "We are moving back to Turlock." She tells us Turlock is a small town in northern California. We miss them when they are no longer part of our neighborhood.

Now to Della. Della's family *loves* to drink Pepsi. Every day, Della walks to the corner store to get a six-pack or two of Pepsi. Many times, I go with her, and sometimes her mom invites me to stay for a meal. "Sharon, go ask your mother if you can stay for dinner." My mother says, "Yes, and remember to put the serviette in your lap." Mother always reminds me about proper etiquette. I have dinner around Della's large family kitchen table where everyone speaks English and Spanish. I drink Pepsi with them, and this is a real treat because at my house, we drink only milk with our meals. In my family, we each get only one bottle of soda a week, and we usually drink that while watching *77 Sunset Strip* on Friday nights.

I watch Della make tamales at Christmas with her mother and sister. The cooking chili peppers make my eyes burn. I sometimes play catch with her older brother, Richard. He is cute, and I develop a crush on him.

summer days and halloween

One summer Della's older sister, Anita, gets all the neighborhood kids together for different activities. We act in plays wearing our mothers' old scarves, hats, dresses and wobble in high heel shoes. One day, we go door-to-door to collect donations for the City of Hope, a well-known nearby hospital. That day is *so, so* hot. It must be at least 106 degrees! And we are *so, so* thirsty. We end up taking the donated money, a total of eighty-five cents, to Young's corner market to buy two big bottles of soda. We feel guilty for a while, but *ah*, the soda is so refreshing! There are days when we play card games and board games too. In September, we pick neighbors' flowers to create our own bouquets to present to our new teachers.

In October, Anita asks, "Who is going to be the brave one to snatch a pomegranate for all of us to share?" We decide who is going to sneak into the Morgan's front yard across the street and snatch fruit from their pomegranate tree. Though there are a lot of us hiding behind the Morgan's bushes, we elect Billy to swipe the red tasty fruit. The juicy seeds leave reddish-purple all over our lips and tongues. Our mothers must surely know what we have been up to!

At the end of the month, we have a Halloween costume contest. We all trick-or-treat together. Each person at every house we knock on has to vote for his or her favorite homemade costume. I do not win; in fact, I don't even get *one* vote. Anita tells me I cannot be in the contest because my costume is not homemade. I dress all in white and put on a white navy hat. I am a sailor! One woman makes me happy when she shouts down the walkway as we leave her house, "Handmade or not, you get my vote because you make the cutest sailor girl!"

elderly people

On my block live many elderly people. Most of the women live by themselves because their husbands have died. There is Mrs. Pier, Mrs. Cozart, Mrs. Potter and Mrs. Foster. They are all thin with gray hair except for Mrs. Pier who is short and stout. I like that there are elderly people nearby. I only see my grandmother part time. She lives in Canada, but in the winter when it is cold and snowy, she comes to California. She stays with us sometimes but more often rents a house or apartment for a few months.

One time though, she stays at the old Aztec Hotel on the corner of Foothill and Magnolia. I join her there for afternoon tea several days a week after school. We always pour cream from a dainty creamer into our tea and with miniature tongs add a sugar cube or two. I drink from a miniature blue-and-white china teacup that rests upon a saucer that Nanny has brought to me from Canada.

Then there is the colonel next door and Mr. and Mrs. Fiss across the street. The colonel likes to scare all the kids on Halloween with his jump-up skeleton on the front porch. We know the skeleton is behind an old dusty stuffed chair sitting in the corner of the wooden porch, but every year we all scream with delight and terror as we ring the doorbell. We know what's coming!

Mr. and Mrs. Fiss are a very sweet couple. They love sitting on their screened-in front porch and frequently invite me in for lemonade. They teach jokes like "What's black and white and red all over?" Answer: "A newspaper!" Mr. Fiss always has a yellow packet of Chiclets gum in his pocket, and he offers me one piece every time I visit. I visit a lot! They always prepare a special Halloween treat for me. Even when Mr. Fiss dies and Mrs. Fiss moves away, she calls each year to tell me she has a special treat and to come by. The last time I go, a classmate from the next block over—her name is Hope—goes with me, and Mrs. Fiss has a special treat for her too.

Edna Pier, our next-door neighbor, is at least in her eighties or nineties and her voice crackles. Her daughter, Mary, is somewhat old, but she still works. I love Mary Pier's home. Her apartment sits over Edna Pier's garage, and the walls are knotty pine. It's as if she owns her *own* cabin! She is a librarian at the Monrovia Public Library.

Mary comes for dinner sometimes, and then we talk and dry dishes in the kitchen together. Mother is the dishwasher and just listens. I remember when I have my tonsils out. Mary Pier brings me a gift. It is a child's weaving loom with twisty fabric loops, and I make colorful potholders for everyone in my family. "Remember to write a thank-you note to Mary," Mother instructs. "You must always write a thank you note when someone gives you a gift or does something nice for you."

more elderly people

I like all the elderly people in my neighborhood, but there are two men who frighten me. Mr. Voorhees lives on Ivy Street behind our house. We have seven orange trees in our backyard, and Mr. Voorhees has seven boysenberry bushes in his backyard—maybe even more. All I know is that there are *so many* berries! Twisty ivy and curly purple morning glories cover the fence where my brothers, Tim and Bill, create a hole. They take turns creeping through the hole when the berries are ripe. I yell at them, "You two are just like Peter Rabbit stealing carrots from Mr. McGregor's garden!" A few times Mr. Voorhees catches them, but they scamper through the hole in the fence, run into our house through the swinging screen door banging "k'bunk, k'bunk" and laugh their heads off. I hesitantly laugh with them. I later find out that Mr. Voorhees is the grandfather of one of my classmates, Barbara. She tells me, "My grandfather is a fun grandfather and teaches me all kinds of games, like dominoes."

Then there is Mr. Burr. He lives on Myrtle Avenue, but his whole back-yard backs up to our street. We play in an area that is an open field of dirt and weeds. Then another section calls to us like a secret garden. Actually it looks more like a jungle—Tarzan's jungle. Tall trees with vines tower over us kids, twisty branches block the natural pathways, and crows and owls caw and hoot high above our heads. The sun barely shines through. The older kids tell us not to play there—that Mr. Burr is a tall, mean old man who will snag us if he catches us. "You'll be sorry if Mr. Burr catches you," the older kids threaten. Mother calms my fears when later she tells me that Mr. Burr is really a very kind man.

marbles

Collecting smooth and noisy marbles is a favorite pastime. I store peewees, cat's eyes, boulders and purees in a blue and brown leather bag with a pull string. I do not play marbles like most other kids—pitching them into a circle. My brothers, Tim and Bill, teach me a different marble game—one that involves a shoebox.

Who puts marbles together with shoeboxes? However, it quickly becomes a favorite activity. I get a shoebox and toss the lid. I turn the box upside down and draw four oval-shaped doors ranging from a tiny door to a large door on one of the long sides. The hardest part is cutting out the doors, but once this is accomplished, I place a number value over the top of each opening. I write "25" over the smallest opening, "15" over the next smallest, "10" over the second from the largest and "5" over the largest opening. "Let the games begin," I say to myself. I set the box upside down with the four doors facing me. From around five feet away, I pitch a marble towards the box. Darn! After many five-and-ten-pointers, a marble finally rolls through the smallest hole. "Yea, a twenty-five pointer!" I work diligently to earn another twenty-five points, and another and another. However, it is not easy.

I play marbles with all the kids in the neighborhood. They go home and create their own boxes. Like true Olympians, we challenge each other to the "high level sport" of shoebox marbles!

yo-yos

An explosion of great toys comes about during the fifties and sixties. The Hula-Hoop, Barbie doll, Frisbee and Mr. Potato Head are just a few. However, the biggest fad toy is the yo-yo. I purchase my first Duncan yo-yo from the toy store on Myrtle Avenue.

Making the yo-yo go up, down, up, down tests my patience! Soon, however, with much practice, I, along with many other kids on the block, can perform several tricks such as shoot the moon, rock the cradle, zip around the world and walk the dog. A few years later, an inventor creates a yo-yo that lights up when performing a trick. Yo-yo tricks with blinking lights are so cool.

jacks

I have a little red bag that holds ten jacks and a small rubber ball. Most of us kids play jacks on the sidewalk in front of one of our houses. After the ten jacks are gently scattered, we take turns letting the ball bounce once and then pick up one jack at a time. If we are successful at picking up all ten jacks, one at a time and each with one bounce, we move to "twos." With the "twosies", we pick up two jacks at once while still letting the ball bounce only once.

If we miss the pickup, then it is another person's turn. We work through the "threesies," "foursies" and on up to ten. When two jacks touch each other while being scattered, we pick them up, bring them to our lips, kiss them and re-toss them. We play jacks for hours.

toot, toot, jingle, jingle, ding dong

Every afternoon we hear "toot, toot." It is the whistle of the Helms Bakery truck making its rounds. The Helms creamy-yellow panel truck is a bakery on wheels. When we hear the "toot, toot," just about every mom and kid on the block runs out with money in their hands to make a purchase. The Helms driver exits his truck, walks to the back, opens the two back doors, slides out the many wooden drawers full of donuts and asks, "What would you like today—glazed, powdered sugar or jelly-filled?" The Helms Bakery man also carries a variety of fresh-baked breads, pies and cakes. How lucky we are to have fresh treats brought practically to our door. It is a sad day when the "toot, toot" whistle is no more. Big supermarkets open up all over and carry the baked goods at cheaper prices, and Helms can no longer afford the gasoline for all their trucks.

After a few hours, we hear a little musical jingle in the air. It's the ice-cream man! We especially look forward to the ice-cream truck during the hot summer months. The orange sherbet push-ups and Fudgcicles are favorites, but there are many other flavors, shapes and sizes of refreshing popsicles and ice cream as well. While we wait, we kids sing a song we learned in school:

Here comes the ice-cream man.
His truck is spic and span.
He rings his bell, so we can tell,
Here comes the ice-cream man.

Later we all shout, "I scream, you scream, we all scream for ice cream!"

☙❧

It is the fifties and while most moms are still full-time homemakers, some moms venture from the house to take jobs outside the home. My mother becomes an Avon lady. She goes door-to-door taking orders for make-up. The company has a commercial on the television: "Ding dong, Avon calling." I can tell Mother loves this little bit of freedom and having her own spending money.

Many times I accompany her as she delivers the small white bags filled with make-up, perfumes, lipsticks, powders, hand creams and rouge. Before too long, *many* items clutter the top of our own bathroom's built-in vanity as Avon introduces more products. Once a week it is my job to dust all the little bottles, jars, tubes and compacts that sit upon a mirrored tray.

saturday matinees

I have to tell you about Anna. She is Scandinavian with fair skin, blond hair and blue eyes. We have been friends since first grade. On most Saturdays, we go to the Lyric Theater. Her mother drives Anna to my house. Then we walk to Young's corner market to spend our quarter on Milk Duds, candy cigarettes, Jujubes, Necco wafers and other candies. Mr. Young puts our candy in brown paper bags. We each grab our own bag and walk swiftly to the theater. The doors open at 11:30 a.m. for the first show at noon.

    As we wait in line, we visit other kids from Mayflower School. Anna and I each have twenty-five cents for our ticket. It is twenty-five cents for kids twelve and under. Some older kids know they are to pay thirty-five cents, but they lie so they can enter for twenty-five cents. (Once, two older kids ask us to buy their tickets for them. The manager catches us, but we are not in trouble. The two older kids are mad because they have to pay the extra ten cents.)

The woman in the glass booth calls out, "That will be twenty-five cents, please." We buy our tickets and giggle as we enter the theater passing the long lines of kids waiting to buy popcorn and candy. Through the tall swinging theater doors, we enter and head to our favorite spot halfway down the aisle and in the middle. The huge curtains and the gigantic floral patterns on the carpet make us feel majestic.

Soon the lights dim, and the usher—in his red button cap and red vest with gold buttons—shines his flashlight on all the kids and orders, "Keep your feet off the row of chairs in front of you!" Anna and I giggle. We think he looks like an organ grinder's monkey in his uniform. The curtains open, the Loony Tunes melody begins and we are ready to be entertained for the next three hours. First the cartoon plays, and then the feature film begins. The loudness and length of the applause rates the enjoyment level of what we have just seen on the big screen. Between the two movie times, there is a drawing from the local toy store. We anxiously look at our tickets as the manager calls out the winning numbers. We have three chances to win—we *never* win.

the big m

I love going to Anna's house. She lives on El Nido at the foot of the San Gabriel Mountain range. From Anna's street, you can see the huge cement M on the hill above her house. It stands for Monrovia. Every night, the Big M is lit up for all to see, like the town's beacon. When the Monrovia High School football team wins its Friday night game, only the V in the middle part of the M is lit. Victory! If the entire M is lit, it signals defeat.

    Anna and I hike to the Big M, but first we tie up her pet beagle. We do not want Jingles to follow us. We collect our snacks of kumquats and loquats from the trees in her front yard. We fill our pockets with them, so we have both hands free for the hike. We walk just five houses north, and then the dirt and rocky climb begins. We carefully help each other put our feet securely on each rock and each dirt shelf until we make it to the top. With a few scratches and scrapes here and there, we sit on the "shoulders" of the Big M taking in the view of the San Gabriel Valley below.

We see the skyscrapers of Los Angeles and even Santa Catalina Island—twenty-six miles across the sea. It is the perfect place to sit, talk, eat kumquats and loquats—we spit the loquat seeds down the hill—and point out landmarks. We see the Big Sky Drive-In movie screen down Peck Road near Irwindale Avenue. We recognize the steeple at St. Luke's Episcopal Church where I am confirmed. We see the Santa Anita Race Track where Father always visits opening day to bet on the horses, and we know the clump of trees next to the racetrack is the arboretum. "I bet we could see the Rose Parade on Colorado Boulevard if we sat here on New Year's Day," giggles Anna.

The city of Irwindale has the rock quarry, El Monte has the San Bernardino Freeway, and Monrovia's Huntington Boulevard is part of the famous Route 66. Here sit two eleven-year-old girls atop a cement M on the side of a mountain overlooking life below—content to while away the hours in one another's company.

the happiest place on earth

If you live in Southern California, most likely you have been to Disneyland at least once. It is about an hour's drive from our house, and the anticipation of spending the day at Disneyland is so exciting! Often I go with Anna's family. We are excited just pulling into the parking lot. We are even more excited just getting on the tram that carries everyone to the entrance gates. We can see through the fences that people have already purchased Mickey and Minnie hats to wear around the park.

Once Anna's father purchases our tickets, he immediately announces, "Here's ten dollars for each of you girls to spend on anything you want to buy." Anna's parents are always so generous. We then have a big decision to make. Where do we go first—Frontierland, Fantasyland, Tomorrowland or Adventureland? And which tickets do we use first? Our ticket books come with passes labeled with A, B, C, D or E. The E rides are the best!

We decide to start our day in a theater with "Great Moments with Mr. Lincoln." Abraham Lincoln addresses the audience with his famous speech. He is not a man dressed up acting the part, rather "he" is a mechanical mannequin that sits then stands as he delivers his speech. We chuckle when we hear behind us an elderly woman with a southern drawl muse, "That man must get awfully tired doing that all day!"

Next, we stroll up Main Street past gift shops, the magic shop and an old country store where we pick up antique party-line phones and listen to gossiping women. We purchase a pickle from the store's pickle barrel. It is crunchy and sour, and the juice drips down our arms as we scramble to eat it. We have to hurry for fear we might miss something, like spotting Annette Funicello, our favorite member of the *Mickey Mouse Club* television show, walking up Main Street. We pass the candy store but decide to wait to purchase treats until the end of the day on our way out of the park.

The Tiki Room, where parrots sing to us, is a favorite and so is the Swiss Family Robinson Treehouse. Jungle Boat Ride always has funny tour guides who convince everyone that there are *real* alligators and hippos in the water. Some of us get drenched as we pass under a waterfall. Drums beat as we navigate by skulls on the banks of the river. By the time the boat ride is over, we feel as though we have been on a great safari adventure.

Mr. Toad's Wild Ride, Alice's Swirling Teacups—"Oh, Anna, I think I'm going to be sick!"—and the sky rides are next. We board another boat and sing a happy tune, "It's a Small World After All" as we "sail" around the world. We notice the long line for the miniature cars as we head to Matterhorn Mountain. Its line is long too, but for this, we wait. It is the best roller coaster ride in the world! We want to stay on it all day. The line for the submarine is long as well, so we decide to enter America the Beautiful. There we stand in a big room with huge screens all around us. We take a 360-degree tour across America through something called cinematography. Sometimes we feel like we are on an airplane or in a wagon traveling across a covered bridge. There is no mistaking it. We *are* on the back of a red fire engine truck as it swerves down a crooked street in San Francisco! Now it is Anna's turn to say, "Oh, Sharon, I think I'm going to be sick!"

We finish our day taking part in a vaudeville show while eating peanuts and drinking sodas. With my ten dollars, I decide on a purchase from the glassblower's shop for Mother—a beautiful pink piano that sits among other glass objects—swans, castles, birds and harps. At 9:00 p.m., Tinker Bell flies from the castle to the Matterhorn, and fireworks light up the sky. We hear "oohs" and "aahs" throughout the park.

We join Anna's parents at Carnation Gardens then wearily walk back down Main Street. We purchase taffy-swirled suckers and fudge that candy makers create before our very eyes. We exit the main gates sleepily and board the trams that return us to Anna's turquois family station wagon. It has been a long but *very* fun day.

hidden valley

"Hi, Sharon Hammond Eggs!"
"Hi, Lisa Flower!"

This is how my friend Lisa and I greet one another on the playground at Mayflower School. Lisa lives in Hidden Valley about one mile north of our school. Walking home to her house after school is like going on a hike. The scenery we pass is very lush, woodsy and secluded. As we trek up the hill and wind our way around several blocks, we sing and whistle Girl Scout songs.

When we reach Lisa's large beautiful home we see deer grazing alongside it. Lisa's mother welcomes us in and gives us oranges for a snack. Lisa educates me in the fine art of eating them properly. First, we slice an orange in half. While we squeeze the halves this way and that, we purse our lips and use our top teeth and tongue to suck out the juice. Once most of the juice is out, we invert the half so that each section flips to the outer edge of the skin.

With our bottom teeth, we scoop out the pulp around each half. We have now successfully eaten the *whole* orange.

It is at Lisa's house too that I eat my first artichoke. We need more teeth maneuvers for this funny looking vegetable. After the artichoke boils, we carefully peel off each leaf, dip it in butter or mayonnaise, add shakes of salt and scrape the artichoke flesh off with our bottom teeth. It sure seems like a lot of work for so little food, but we both agree that it is worth it.

Sometimes I stay overnight at Lisa's, and sometimes she sleeps over at my house. In the middle of one night at her house, I shake Lisa anxiously. "Lisa, wake up! I can't breathe!" Her pet cat sneaks in to sleep at the foot of the bed, and I end up having a severe asthma attack. After consulting with my parents over the phone, Lisa's father drives me home at one o'clock in the morning.

Except for asthma attacks, it is always fun at Lisa's house. We explore "clay dam" just around the corner from her house, and it is here we encounter a coiled snake sunning itself just inches from our feet. We freeze in our tracks for a few seconds before simultaneously yelling, "Run!" We take off screaming through the rocks, manzanita plants and clay. We scurry up the hill to search for *"gold"* and special rocks, and we even make the climb to Gold Hill where several houses overlook the valley.

One late morning after exploring, we return to Lisa's house, and her father says in a hushed voice, "Girls, come with me. I want to show you something." We follow Lisa's father down the hallway, through the living room and into the back bedroom. He opens the curtains and says, "Be quiet, but take a look." We peer through the curtains, and our eyes get wide as saucers. The neighbors, who have been given use of the pool at any time, are sunbathing—and they are *very* naked! Lisa and I clasp our hands over our mouths and giggle all the way back to the other end of the house. We can hardly believe what we have seen. Lisa finds out later and explains, "Those neighbors are from Europe, and they believe that nude sunbathing is perfectly acceptable." We just shake our heads in amazement.

One day we do a horrible thing. We do not realize it is horrible at the time. We think we are doing a good thing. There is a huge beehive on the tree at the foot of Lisa's driveway. Bees are swarming everywhere. Along with several neighborhood kids, we try with all our might to knock the swarming house down. We use rocks, sticks and anything else we can find. Yet the beehive does not budge. Breathlessly, we run inside Lisa's house to escape the swarm of bees now chasing after us! Her parents inquire, "What's all this commotion about?" We hurriedly tell them our plight, and then we get a mini lecture about how we should not disrupt nature.

We both love the movie, *Parent Trap* with actress Haley Mills, and we learn the theme song, "Let's Get Together." We play the record hundreds of times and perform for her parents and friends one Friday night. We move our lips to the music and pretend that we are singing and playing guitars on a stage. We soak up their applause.

Other things about Lisa: She and her brother, Ted, are good at playing the piano. Because of Lisa, I convince my parents to let me take piano lessons too. Lisa then continues with cello lessons. I do not understand why she chooses the cello. It is so big and clunky. However, she loves it and plays it beautifully. Later, Lisa plays in several well-known symphonies throughout the Los Angeles area. I continue with guitar. It is because I want to be a folk singer and be in a group like Peter, Paul and Mary. I learn a few chords and a few songs, only to play and sing with my friend Janice for a few years.

Once there is a fire in the mountains above Monrovia. The frightening flames are close to Lisa's house. Her family hoses down the roof and evacuates. Thankfully, firefighters save their house and many others.

I remember when Lisa walks by my house with a new purchase from the record store, "Chain Gang" by Sam Cooke. It's currently a big hit heard constantly on the radio. Everyone likes to grunt the "ooh, aah!" part.

Lisa reminds me, "Do you remember that time at your house when my mother comes by with a bag of training bras? She wants me to try them on at your house. I am mortified!" To Lisa's mother, it seems irrelevant that our breasts are the size of swollen mosquito bites.

Soon, we come to the end of our elementary years, and Lisa and I move on to junior high school. We are assigned to different classes, so we do not see each other as much. In high school, we get together a few times, but again, we do not have any classes together. Our lives continue in different directions, but to this day, we still consider each other the dearest of childhood friends.

lifesavers

Linda moves into our neighborhood in 1960. She and her family are from Canada. I tell her my family is from Canada too, and so we bond instantly. We ride bikes together, go for walks and wait at the school bus stop together. I love to eat her grandmother's homemade cinnamon rolls! The aroma of cinnamon and sugar wafting from the kitchen is heavenly. "Linda," I plead, "Do you think Grandmother Nelson would mind if we have just *one* more cinnamon roll?"

On Saturdays, we go window-shopping on Myrtle Avenue. One Saturday in particular we will never forget. We walk up Myrtle Avenue past the stores, the Leven Oaks Hotel, the U.S. National Bank and the First Presbyterian Church. We then enter into the residential neighborhood of Myrtle Avenue. As we near a two-story house, we see a toddler step out of the second-story window and climb into a flower box just above the first floor's roofline. The baby trips, falls out of the flower box and rolls down the roof.

Linda and I both gasp but miraculously spring into action as we scramble across the lawn just in time. Together we join arms and hands to break the toddler's fall. Apparently, the mother, who just rented the second story apartment, is exhausted from the move and falls asleep believing her child to be asleep too. She runs down the stairs and out the front door when she hears screams and crying. She is grateful for our heroic feat.

There is one odd thing. A woman across the street waters her lawn with a hose and is oblivious to the whole ordeal. She waters away with a blank solemn look on her face. It's as though she is not there. However, just at the right time, Linda and I are there.

clifton junior high school

I am almost twelve years old when I start seventh grade at Clifton Junior High School. Promoted students not only transfer here from Mayflower School but from Plymouth, Monroe, Wild Rose, Santa Fe and Bradoaks elementary schools as well. We have six different classrooms to go to throughout the day, but we always start and end in our assigned homeroom. Mr. McCullough is my homeroom teacher. He tells the class he started out as a school janitor before becoming a teacher. He tells the funniest jokes like when he is driving and notices a sign that says "Stop Ahead." Mr. McCullough tells us he always stops, gets out of his car, looks around, but he never finds "a head!"

In junior high, we must complete our class work and homework each day to avoid demerits. We sit respectfully in our chairs or face demerits—three demerits and it is the walk of shame to the principal's office. It is at Clifton that I learn the preamble to the U.S. Constitution, learn how to write a term paper and discover that I am good at making baskets from the free-throw line in physical education. At last, a team captain wants me on *her* team!

We change into green uniforms for P.E. class, undress and shower in front of other girls. This takes getting used to. We even have to wrap a towel around us after showering and report to the teacher with our student number so she knows we showered. Do you know how hard it is after class to undress, shower, report to the teacher, get your locker opened, put deodorant on, get dressed, comb your hair, gather up your books and make it to the next class all under twelve minutes? We holler, "WE NEED MORE TIME!"

It is at Clifton that I learn what the word "assassination" means. One day in November, the bells and teachers tell us to return to our homeroom *immediately*. Many of us already know why. The principal comes over the intercom to relay the tragic news: "President Kennedy was assassinated today in Texas." The principal leads us in a moment of silence and then recites a prayer. Eyes start tearing up. School lets out, we go home, and the news is on *every* station. Over and over all three networks— CBS, NBC and ABC show the parade in Texas and the convertible car Mr. President and Mrs. Kennedy are riding in. We hear the gunshots and throngs of people screaming. Americans cry for days, weeks, months even. I never get the image out of my mind of three-year old John-John saluting his father's casket as the funeral procession rolls by.

mother

At times Mother is distant—far away in another time, another land. To drown out her thoughts, she plays opera and classical music on the console record player in our small den. Also in this room is the upright piano on which I take lessons and a hide-in-the-wall bed that rolls out when needed. The windows are always open with a fresh breeze drifting through the sheer curtains. I am sure, to my embarrassment, that all the neighbors can hear this loud foreign music emitting out of our den on Encinitas.

What are they thinking? Is my mother crazy? This is not the music other neighbors listen to. And the books—art books, music books, psychology books, books on spirituality, poetry and most notably, works by Carl Sandburg. There are stacks of papers and magazines, and cigarette butts fill every ashtray to the brim! I think, "Why is my mother so different from the other mothers?"

Mother's alarm sounds at 5:00 a.m. This is when she enjoys her quiet reading time. She is always beautifully dressed for the day, whether she is wearing a soft blue cotton dress that cinches in the middle on her tiny waist or a pair of pedal pushers with a sleeveless button-down blouse. My friends think her hair and facial expressions resemble those of Lauren Bacall, a famous movie star.

Mother loves musicals in the same way she devours opera and classical music. She and Father take me to my first musical at Grauman's Chinese Theatre in Hollywood to see *West Side Story*. I fall madly in love with the character playing Bernardo, the leader of a Puerto Rican gang calling themselves the Sharks. They fight and dance their way through the movie along with the Jets, a New York gang. (Mother loves the dancing; she was a tap and modern dancer during her youth.) Most of the fights are because Tony of the Jets has fallen in love with Maria. Bernardo is Maria's big brother, and he is very protective of her. I buy the album that same week along with the piano music of all the songs. "Tonight" is the first song I learn to play on the piano, but my favorite one to perform is "America."

> I like to be in America,
> Okay by me in America.

But back to Mother: She wants all of us to experience opportunities to hear fine music, attend creative plays, visit museums and enjoy operas at the Pasadena Playhouse—during which I usually fall asleep. At my age, I do not realize how fortunate my brothers and I are to have a mother who wants to enrich our lives in this way. Again, I think it is because we are Canadian; Mother grew up in a very formal environment with educated parents and upper-class interests and values. Though moving to casual sunny California is exciting for her, I am sure she often misses the formal ways of her first thirty years of life in Canada.

father

Father has the same routine Monday through Friday. Mother wakes him up at 6:30 a.m. He eats a crunchy shredded wheat biscuit with milk and sugar. Then he has toast and marmalade jam and drinks orange juice and coffee. (One day we have a good laugh when Mother yells, "Ralph, breakfast is ready. It's garbage day!" We all laugh and giggle at what she shouts. She is reminding Father that breakfast is ready, and the garbage cans need to be set out for pickup.) Next, Father dresses for work. Each morning as he pulls out of the driveway in our silvery-blue Super Sport Chevy Impala, he is dressed in a suit, white button-down collared shirt and a tie. He looks so handsome. (Often he is mistaken for the actor, Ronald Reagan.) He waves good-bye as he backs out of the driveway and turns down the street. It is only a twenty-minute drive to the Jet Propulsion Lab (JPL) in Altadena where he works as a quality control inspector.

When Saturdays come, the routine changes. I spend a lot of time with Father in the yards. He mows and I rake. He edges and I sweep. Father gets the sprinklers going, and I love the "che-che-che" sound of the oscillating sprinkler swaying back and forth. I hose down the planter areas and driveway. Everything must look tidy and clean.

Mother cleans the inside of our house. "Stuff" clutters every single room, but each week she dusts, vacuums, changes the sheets and towels, washes the laundry and hangs everything out to dry among our many backyard orange trees. "We always have the freshest smelling laundry," beams Father.

On Sunday afternoons, my father and I go for a drive—"a Sunday drive." We drive down Foothill Boulevard to Santa Anita and turn right toward the mountains. We marvel at all the beautifully landscaped homes in Arcadia and dream of living there. Sometimes though, we stay in our town and drive up to Monrovia Canyon Park. We pass the dam and then enter a beautiful wooded picnic area with hiking trails and a stream. We park and look out over the vast San Gabriel Valley below.

Still, other times we drive through Bradbury Estates where movie stars are rumored to live. Each house sits on acres of land. White split-rail fences and horses abound. Besides working part time at the Monrovia Bakery on Myrtle Avenue, my auntie Olla is a nanny to a little boy whose family raises horses there. He suffers with asthma just like me. He is allergic to the horses! We drive by their home and think how lucky she is to work in such a beautiful house.

To conclude our day, we drive down Huntington Boulevard to the Foster's Freeze. No Sunday drive would ever be complete without a vanilla cone dipped in chocolate.

brother tim

I cannot believe at nine years old,
Tim is a "businessman."

I cannot believe at nine years old,
Tim buys his first bike.

I cannot believe at nine years old,
Tim makes $100 in tips at Christmas time.

My brother Tim is amazing. He works each day after school delivering newspapers. Tim's paper route is number twenty-two. He loops a canvas bag over the handlebars of his bike and quickly stuffs his folded papers in the bag. Off he goes! First, he delivers to the fire department, the police department and city hall. Next, he tosses the papers to homes on and around Ivy, Shamrock, Lime, Lemon and Olive streets. He delivers the *Monrovia News Post* to 130 customers every day. Just before

Christmas, he sends each of his customers a Christmas card and hand delivers the newspaper with a red ribbon tied around it. This is how he earns about $100 in tips around the holiday. He explains, "It's my personal touch."

When Tim is thirteen years old, he gets another job at the *Monrovia News Post*. He pours molten lead to make slugs for the Linotype machines. He still delivers newspapers, but at seventeen years old, he becomes a district manager as well. Tim is a respectable "businessman" who earns trips to San Diego, Disneyland, San Francisco, Big Bear and Long Beach.

I think Tim is lucky, because he always has money and gets to take fun trips. One year he says "Happy Birthday Toots"—his nickname for me, and gives me a whole five dollars. I immediately run down to Mc Bratney's, the local department store, to buy a new paisley blouse. I admire my brother and can hardly wait until I can work. When I start work, I will save for a car just like Tim.

Tim's first car is a 1957 Ford Fairlane 500. After owning it for a while, he sells it and buys a 1960 Chevy Impala. The Chevy is black with red interior. Later he sells the Chevy to a friend named Alan and purchases a blue Volkswagen Beetle. Ronnie and Dick, Tim's two best friends, drive "Bugs" as well. Ronnie's is beige and Dick's is black. A big grin appears on my face when all three drive up and park in front of our house—radios blasting with surfing music.

Tim, Ronnie, Dick and another friend named Treg, take a tour of the Western United States in Ronnie's Volkswagen. They travel as far as Mount Rushmore and eat buffalo steaks at a "hoity-toity" lodge where people get all dressed up for dinner.

Tim's adventures never stop. He and friend Alan buy ten-speed bikes and together bicycle 480 miles north to

San Francisco. However, they get sick and have to take a bus home. Great is their disappointment that the adventure ends on a Greyhound bus.

At eighteen years old, Tim enrolls at Citrus Junior College in Azusa. He works many jobs to put himself through school before transferring to Humboldt State in northern California. He leaves the newspaper business and works for California Water and Telephone, Myrtle Avenue Lumber, California Hardware Company and Union Pacific Railroad.

In 1965, rather than face a draft notice from the government, Tim decides to join the marine reserves. It is after boot camp in San Diego and firing training at Camp Pendleton that Tim returns to college. While working in the sawmills of Humboldt county, he earns a bachelor's degree in business management. He continues to earn his master's degree in 1970 while attending night school. Mother and Father are proud of Tim. He has put himself through six years of college with only a $100 loan from them, and he pays that back right away.

Tim is self-sufficient from a very early age and takes pride in being able to take care of himself. I take after my brother Tim.

I too love to work. My first job at fifteen-and-a-half is cleaning reel-to-reel films at the Monrovia Public Library after school. At sixteen, I work at the *Monrovia News Post* before school categorizing ticker tape from the Associated Press machine—for typesetting the day's stories. Later, I work as a "soda jerk" or rather a waitress at Steuve's Ice-Cream Rendezvous. It is my favorite job, since I love serving happy people ice cream and soda concoctions, and the tips help when Father and I purchase my first car—a 1965 silver-blue Ford Mustang.

I have saved $1000 and Father loans me $400. I pay Father back with my summer pay, and often Tim says, "Come on, Toots. Let's practice your driving." My new car is a three-speed stick shift, and using a clutch is very tricky. Thankfully, Tim is patient while teaching me to drive.

brother bill

My brother Bill is not a bad person, but his choices seem to get him into trouble. Mother and Father often quarrel about how to discipline him. I am embarrassed when my parents argue about Bill; I go around and close all the windows so the neighbors won't hear.

Bill makes me laugh. Actually, he makes *all* of us laugh with his funny stories and jokes. He spends time with me to make up for what he thinks I am missing. (He is concerned about the disagreements I am witness to.) We have some good times together, and I am excited when he invites me to go places with him.

We go for hamburgers and milk shakes at Rod's Diner in Arcadia and to the drive-in movie theater to see *It's a Mad, Mad, Mad, Mad World*. We spend an evening at Disneyland, and he teaches me my first three chords on the guitar. After Bill sees the movie, *My Fair Lady* with his girlfriend, Gloria, he asks me to repeat, "The ra-a-ain in Spa-a-ain falls mai-ain-ly on the plai- ains." I do not know what Bill is talking about, but I practice these words until I get the enunciation just right.

Speaking of his girlfriend, Gloria and Bill love to dance, and they win many dance contests on Friday nights. I like Gloria. For one of my birthdays, she buys me a plastic turquoise wallet with a picture of Elvis painted on it. Her mother, June, creates many ceramic objects for me. Over time, she makes a snowman, Santa, Santa's boot, two Christmas angels—the boy angel is holding a slingshot behind his back—and a jewelry box with pink rhinestones. These remain some of my favorite possessions.

When Bill is in high school, he decides it would be best if he not live at our house; another family offers to let him stay with them for a while. Bill still comes by to visit bringing with him funny stories and jokes. Mother and I love his naughty jokes! I retell all the jokes to my friends the next day at school.

Bill is very intelligent, but he does not like school. He does not graduate from Monrovia High School; later he earns a GED from a night school in Palm Springs. He is there to work at the Thunderbird Club as a busboy, the first of many interesting places of employment. Bill seems to have money all the time from all the different restaurants where he works—from Duarte's Zanzibar to Monrovia's My Old Kentucky Home, where they make the *best* corn fritters. "Bill runs with a 'fast' crowd," Father says a bit worried. He never quite understands Bill; Mother always does. "Bill just marches to a different drummer," Mother always says.

Mother and Bill have a special connection. They seem to understand each other and spend hours trying to make sense of their world. They sit, smoke and talk about art, music, plays, their love of antiques and Europe. Bill visits

Europe; I do not know why or with whom, but when he returns he brings back gifts for everyone. Bill is always thinking of others especially Mother and me. I think he worries about us, and Mother worries about Bill, wondering if he has it worse than others do ever since a car hit him at the age of nine while crossing Foothill Boulevard. He spent days in the hospital. Or did he suffer brain damage during a Sunday school pool party when some girls plugged in a stereo and he stepped on the cord with wet feet? There is a heavy sorrow in her voice as Mother muses, "I guess we'll never know."

I do know that as an adult, Bill is proud of his success in advertising and sales, and he is the happiest when he marries and has a little boy named Jeff. He never stops talking about Jeff, and we are all so happy for Bill—that he seems genuinely happy. Then difficulties arise and new challenges begin. As an extremely sensitive person, Bill faces many trials in life. Nevertheless, his kindness, generosity and caring are always with me. I carry his love deep in my heart.

extended family

With brothers six and seven years older, at times it feels like I am an only child. I have no cousins in the United States; my Auntie Olla never marries, Auntie Doris is divorced with no children and Auntie Retta and Uncle Bill have no children either. My aunts and uncle become the center of my world, and I imagine my brothers and I are the center of their world as well.

    Mother and Father usually host holiday and birthday dinners. I remember one of my birthdays in particular. First, we gather in the living room for before-dinner drinks. Family members sip wine from their crystal glasses, while I sit nestled between two of my aunties on our olive green velvet sofa. I drink Canada Dry ginger ale from my own little wine glass. Large paintings of Blue Boy and Pinkie Lee look down upon us from each side of the fireplace. The cherry wood coffee table displays a large yellow amber ashtray—of which I have cleaned out all the cigarette butts before our company arrives, a wooden bowl full of nuts—complete with silver-plated nutcracker and pick, cocktail napkins and several issues of U.S. News and World Report.

I sit quietly and listen intently to the grown-up conversations formally taking place around politics and religion. There is much discussion and heated debates. Soon we sit down for Mother's traditional dinner of roast beef, mashed potatoes, green beans, homemade rolls and salad. Father pours more wine; I get a glass of milk. Mother prepares delicious desserts, and on this birthday, she bakes an angel food cake and covers it with multiple colors of swirled whipped cream. Mother serves it with chocolate ice cream—my favorite. Everyone sings "Happy Birthday" to me.

Once again, we retire to the living room where Mother serves port wine. Again, I squeeze in between my aunties, and I drink a second glass of ginger ale, which is more than the regular allowance of one soda per week. However, this is a special occasion. Though the atmosphere is prim and proper, there is laughter—perhaps the wine aids in the delight. Next, I open my presents. Mother wraps my present in her "signature" wrap—tissue paper with the ends taped to the top and curly ribbon holding it together. This year Father and Mother buy me several dresses for school. I wear them proudly to school with white socks and black and white saddle shoes.

My aunts and Uncle Bill always give me gift money. Mother teaches me not to say, "Thank you for the five dollars!" Rather I am to respond, "Thank you so much for the gift money." I am *very* thankful for the gift money; I save it in the U.S. National Bank on the corner of Foothill Boulevard and Myrtle Avenue. Before the evening ends, Uncle Bill and I play card games we have been playing for as long as I can remember—Rummy and Concentration. With a wink and a grin Uncle Bill exclaims, "Oh you beat me again, Sharon!"

Birthday and holiday dinners with extended family create comfort and joy throughout my growing-up years.

everyone goes to church

It seems that everyone in Monrovia goes to church on Sundays. Lisa, Dionne, Mary and I attend St. Luke's Episcopal Church. Other friends and classmates attend various other houses of worship. A large group of popular kids goes to First Presbyterian. Others are members of The First Nazarene. Linda and her parents drive to a non-denominational church in Duarte, a neighboring town. Some kids are Mormon; some are Baptist. Beth and Jassy are Catholic. They go to confession on Saturday before they attend church on Sunday. Beth tells me if she swears or does bad things after confession, she cannot go to church on Sunday. Twins Ed, Suzie and their older twin sisters are Lutheran.

After the very formal and structured Episcopalian service, I visit the community room where there is a display case of Christian jewelry. I like to look at the Saint Christopher necklaces and the small gold crosses with tiny pearls. One of the crosses has a diamond at the top.

When I peer carefully into it with one eye, I see The Lord's Prayer written. How can this be? I guess the "diamond" is really a piece of magnifying glass. Anyway, it is magical for me. I cry with delight when Mother and Father buy this necklace for my thirteenth birthday. I wear it proudly and show it off to everyone.

Then one day all hell breaks loose. The churches face competition. Of *all* things, stores begin to stay open on Sundays! The Eastland Shopping Center in West Covina is the biggest draw. They have a Muscatel's variety store and a Clifton's Cafeteria and many other shops. People now spend hours on Sunday buying housewares, eating lunch in the mall and window-shopping. For some, it is the highlight of their week. "Heaven help the churches!" I shout out during one of our formal Sunday afternoon dinners. Father, Mother, Tim and Bill all laugh hysterically at my remark, and I giggle because I have said something that makes my family laugh.

four close friends

My parents purchase a large Tudor-style home on Hillcrest Boulevard during my first week of high school. I now have a large bedroom with crank-out windows on two full walls and a red rotary-dial phone that comes with the room. I cannot count the number of conversations or the minutes spent on this phone with friends during my four years of high school.

I know Jassy from junior high school, but we do not become friends until our assignment to the same physical education class at Monrovia High School. Here we meet Beth who transfers to MHS from a private catholic school.

The three of us are as different as night and day, but somehow we bond all through high school. Jassy is a beautiful mix of Dutch and Indonesian descent and has three sisters and one brother who are all close in age. Her mother is a widow; Jassy's father has passed away. Going to Jassy's house is always exciting for me. Bill and Tim live on their own now, and often my house feels almost *too* quiet. At Jassy's house, there is so much activity! Monica, Linda, Hedy and Edwin are Jassy's siblings, and there always seem to be rousing happenings going on in their house; I thrive on this! Jassy's house is bursting with energy, and at times, I envy the closeness she shares with her sisters and brother.

I remember a time when Jassy irons Hedy's hair. Hedy's hair hangs down to her waist. To keep it smooth, silky and straight, Jassy irons her hair regularly with a steam iron on the ironing board. Unbelievable! And Jassy and Hedy share the same birth date exactly one year apart. The two of them always host a huge birthday party with many friends. Jassy's mother cooks all day for the big event.

Everyone loves the ethnic food—the chicken satay with peanut sauce is a favorite. Bean sprouts and egg rolls are also on the menu. Her mother is a character and joins in with the fun. She even involves the guests in party games. (She has this skill because, as a Stanley distributor, she sponsors home parties, and she involves everyone in talking and having a good time before she presents her product line.)

Of course, Jassy and Hedy look like they have stepped off a glamour magazine cover. They spend hours shopping, selecting the right dress, jewelry and makeup for the birthday festivities. Jassy's nails display a perfect manicure. I ask Jassy, "Why do you need to spend all this time getting ready? You can grab anything off any clothing rack and look great in it!" As for me, I do not like shopping for clothes; nothing ever seems to fit right. Jassy browses in one store for hours; I am done in five minutes!

Beth is cute, short and petite and shows pride in her Italian heritage. She is the middle child in her family with one older brother and one younger brother. I learn quickly that Beth's parents assign her many responsibilities because

Life on Encinitas

she is the only daughter. She cleans, cooks and works just as hard in the house as her mother. In spite of these demands, Beth possesses a wonderful sense of humor.

Beth loves jewelry. She "oohs" and "aahs" at every single jewelry window display, especially at Box Jewelers on Myrtle Avenue. Rings and bracelets bother my skin, so I have little interest in even looking at the shiny items that Beth and Jassy too, find so mesmerizing. However, Beth and I do have something in common. We love ice cream, and we devour chocolate!

One rainy day, Beth and I visit Steuve's Ice Cream Rendezvous on Foothill Boulevard where we order our first-ever hot fudge sundae. (This is before I become a waitress there a year later.) The goblet is huge, so we decide to share one sundae. We love this frozen treat so much that the next time we go to Steuve's, we each order our *own* hot fudge sundae, and we each eat every mouthful down to scraping the last bit of chocolate from the bottom of the goblet. We make ourselves sick eating this much ice cream and chocolate. Nevertheless, we still go back repeatedly! It is about this time that Father recognizes Beth and I are always studying our profiles in the mirror and making judgments about our figures. Father declares, "Girls, you just need to eat 'three squares a day' and you will stay healthy and trim."

It is my seventeenth birthday, and Beth and I drive to the grand and magnificent Huntington Hotel in Pasadena. We visit a radio station with the possibility of interviewing Casey Kasem, a popular disk jockey for a human-interest story for the Teen Page of the *Monrovia News Post*. He is not there, so we leave a message and he calls me back. I do not get a story, but I talk to Casey Kasem on the phone for a *whole* ten minutes.

Jassy encourages me to write. "Sharon, why don't you sign up for the journalism class? I think you'll enjoy it." I do, and from there I become a co-teen-page reporter with Donna, another classmate and friend, interview several classmates for human-interest stories, and at one time interview the famous conductor Carmen Dragon. He visits our campus and works with the concert choirs in preparation for a special patriotic program scheduled at Hollywood's Forest Lawn. During the interview, he gives me a famous quote: "If you want to remain young, associate with the young; if you want to die young, try to keep up with them!" The quote becomes part of a full article in the *Monrovia News Post* about Mr. Dragon's visit to our high school.

Linda, our even-tempered friend from Canada, is also part of our group, and together the four of us experience fun times at Monrovia High School. We go to Friday-night football games, attend movies—our favorite is the thriller, *Wait Until Dark* with Audrey Hepburn, and we enjoy folk music at Mentor Alley's Pasadena Ice House. We buy tickets together for the school dances where we gyrate to the Beach Boys, the Beatles and the Rolling Stones. On Friday nights we "TP" boys' houses—we throw toilet paper up in the trees and over the shrubs.

One night we decide to "TP" Tom's house, a classmate and friend of ours who plays piano for the school's concert choirs. We have such a good time "decorating" Tom's front yard until his mother comes out the front door. She is not angry with us though. She shouts out, "Tom is not home. Why don't you come in for a soda?" Tom's mother engages us in conversation, and by the end of the night we all agree, "Tom has the coolest mom!"

Life on Encinitas

Throughout high school, the four of us, Jassy, Beth, Linda and I encourage and support one another in various ways. We share in birthdays, participate in school functions, become involved in several clubs, get excited for Linda when her family welcomes a baby girl and attend plays in which Beth is starring. We celebrate together when Jassy serves as Girl's League vice-president, and I serve in Madquins, a service group consisting of twenty senior girls. Together, we help each other navigate the four years of high school, and to this day, our friendship continues, though now, cell phones, i-Phones and e-mail replace the red rotary-dial phone.

boyfriends

I have three *real* boyfriends during high school: Leon, Warren and Cary.

Leon: My friend Kathy and her family invite me to go to their church on Sunday nights for service and on Wednesday nights for youth group. Because my Episcopal church is formal and subdued, I am attracted to the casual services and friendliness of everyone at this church, a Southern Baptist church located in El Monte. It is here that I get to know a boy named Leon, and he becomes my first boyfriend.

For half a year or so, we are a couple who only see each other on Sunday and Wednesday nights at church. We talk on the phone, and when he gives me his school ring, which is too big for me, I wrap dental tape around it and seal it with nail polish. I wear it proudly to school. Then one day in my first-year Spanish class, a girl named Regina says to me, "So when are you going to get married?" I think,

"Married!" I'm only fourteen years old; I am not thinking of marriage! I break up with Leon and do not have another boyfriend until I am a junior in high school.

Warren: I serve as banner girl manager with another classmate named Kathy, and together we attend parades with the banner girls who march in front of our school's marching band. We carry the first aid kit, make sure the girls all have spotless white shoes minus scuffmarks, and we shout out when they are not in a straight line. We get a lot of exercise following along the parade route with them.

One of the most important parade competitions takes place in Long Beach each year, and this is where I get to know Warren. He plays the trombone in the Monrovia High School marching band and at the awards ceremony that night we hold hands. We are both juniors and enjoy our time in high school. While dating, we go to drive-in movies, enjoy club activities and spend a memorable day with his parents on their boat in Long Beach. Warren takes me to my first jazz concert in Pasadena. We see the Dave Brubeck Quartet and this is where I fall in love with the song "Take Five." The rhythm is very tricky, and Warren impresses me when he plays part of it on the piano. We also attend the opening of the movie, *Hawaii* in Hollywood. (We are a few minutes late because of the heavy traffic on the old curvy Pasadena Freeway.) However, our last big date is the junior/senior prom. His sister-in-law styles my hair that day, I wear a yellow gown and Warren picks me up in his '59 Chevy. We stay out past midnight. When summer comes, we break up. Warren's one true love, Linda, is home from college and they start dating again. A few years later, they marry, and Warren goes on to become a successful family man and business executive.

Life on Encinitas

Cary: It is at an AFS (American Field Service) Christmas party that I meet Cary. Monrovia High School and neighboring Duarte High School decide to host together the AFS party to honor our foreign exchange students. Our exchange students are Anne-Marie from Norway and Pierre from France. They have two foreign exchange students as well, though we have not met them.

My friend Jassy notices a tall, handsome Asian boy and says, "Sharon, go ask that boy over there which country he is from." I approach the tall, handsome Asian boy and do just that. "Hello," I say. "My name is Sharon, and I'm a senior at Monrovia High School. Which country are you from?" He replies with a wry smile, "My name is Cary, and I am the Associated Student Body president at Duarte High School." I feel two inches tall after his remark, but he smiles, we visit for a while and later exchange phone numbers. We date for the next seven months.

Cary has a great sense of humor and seems much older than his seventeen years. He writes on his hand, "Made in Japan." One of my favorite dates with Cary is when we drive to the Los Angeles Airport, lie on our stomachs in a field next to the landing strip and watch the planes fly in. We then sing Beatles songs on the drive home. When we start college, I see Cary infrequently, because now I am dating another boy whom I have met on a blind date. Cary finishes college and becomes a Hollywood actor appearing on television shows and in films.

☙❧

During the summer after graduation, I meet Carl, who becomes my best friend. We date exclusively while we each attend different colleges and marry the next year.

Three-and-a-half years later we are a family of four moving to the San Joaquin Valley to raise our two children. For the next forty years, we call northern California our home, and it is here we help to create fond childhood memories for our own children.

a note from the author

As a member of the writing group, "The Write Bunch," I thank each member for encouraging me to write, write, and write! In meeting and talking at least once a month, each served as an accountability partner in my pursuit of writing *Life on Encinitas*.

I am especially grateful to my loving husband, Carl, and to our faith-based 12-Step program. Here we have both learned to view life through much wiser eyes. I feel so blessed that for today, I can celebrate what is truly valuable regarding precious childhood memories of family and friends.

There were many special times with other dear friends during my childhood and adolescent years: Janice, Karen, Loren, Ed, Tom R., Tom S., Oakley, Jeff, Jim, Nona,

Donna, Kathy, Kim, Ralph, Mary, Melinda, Marilyn and Anne-Marie. Thanks for all the memories.

"The child with a sense of the past is a child with a sense of destiny. The child with a past from which to draw is a rich child."
    Katie Funk Wiebe

Made in the USA
San Bernardino, CA
03 May 2014